KU-310-793

Wheels are a brilliant invention for helping us get around.

Scientists use tools like this powerful microscope to help them discover new things, such as microbes, or germs.

In this modern factory, robots are building cars.

What is Science?

Science means looking at the things around us, measuring them and testing them. This helps us find out how our universe works, and helps scientists find the answers to lots of questions.

Think of a theory

A theory is an idea about how something works. Scientists come up with theories to explain things. For example, a scientist might have a theory that loud music makes people's hearts beat faster.

By watching chimpanzees carefully, scientists have found that they use tools such as sticks to dig out insects to eat.

We can find out how dinosaurs used to live by studying dinosaur fossils – remains that were preserved in rock or soil.

4

Experiments

To test ideas and theories, scientists do experiments. They design them carefully. To test her theory that loud music makes people's hearts beat faster, this scientist has to set up an experiment.

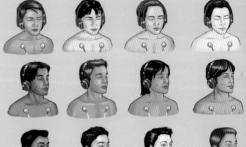

The scientist finds 12 people to experiment on.

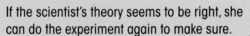

The volunteers are attached to machines that measure their heartbeat. Four people listen to loud music, four hear quiet music and four hear silence. The scientist measures each person's heartbeat. Is there any difference between them?

If the scientist's theory seems to be right, she can do the experiment again to make sure.

Scientists sometimes grow germs such as bacteria in a container called a petri dish. Studying germs helps us understand and control diseases caused by them.

Always changing

Science is not just a big list of facts. Science changes all the time, as scientists find out new things.

This picture shows a computer model of a virus. Viruses are the tiniest types of germs. They attack our cells and make us sick. For many years, scientists thought that viruses were liquid but we now know that they are not.

Scientific Discoveries

This timeline shows some of the most important science discoveries in history.

Galileo drew this sketch of Jupiter and four of its moons after spotting them from his telescope. At first, he thought they were stars.

440–420 BC
Leucippus and Democritus develop the theory that everything around us is made of tiny atoms.

1665
Robert Hooke discovers cells.

1687
Isaac Newton sets out his laws of motion and gravity.

200s BC
Eratosthenes proves the Earth is round. He uses maths to calculate the size of the Earth.

1610
Galileo Galilei discovers moons around the planet Jupiter.

1600
William Gilbert discovers Earth's magnetic field and studies electricity.

AD 700s
Jabir ibn Hayyan (Geber) does the first chemistry experiments.

1510
Copernicus finds out that the planets revolve around the Sun.

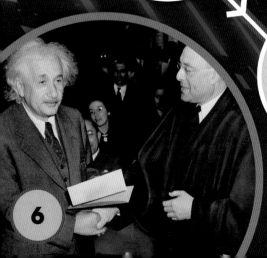

Albert Einstein (far left) is famous for his discoveries about time, space and energy.

6

1928
Alexander Fleming discovers how penicillin can kill germs.

1953
Francis Crick and James Watson discover the structure of DNA and how it works.

1927
Georges Lemaître describes his theory that the universe began with the "Big Bang".

1977
Scientists discover hydrothermal vents on the seabed.

Marie Curie was one of the first people to study radioactivity, or the ability of some elements to give off energy. She also discovered the elements radium and polonium.

1750
Benjamin Franklin captures electricity from lightning in a kite string.

1924
Edwin Hubble discovers galaxies beyond our own, the Milky Way.

2001
Scientists make the first map of human genes.

1800
Frederick William Herschel discovers infrared light while studying the temperature of visible light.

1916
Einstein's Theory of General Relativity describes gravity, space and time.

Isaac Newton made important discoveries about light, gravity and motion. This picture shows him using a type of glass to study light rays.

1859
Charles Darwin publishes his Theory of Natural Selection.

1869
Dmitri Mendeleev creates the periodic table of the elements.

What is Technology?

Technology doesn't just mean modern, electronic things. It can mean any useful machine or invention. For thousands of years, humans have invented things to help us do jobs, make things and move around.

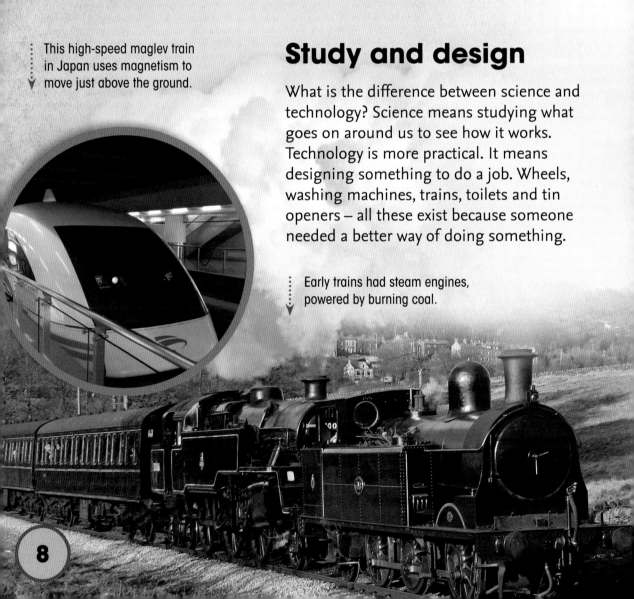

This high-speed maglev train in Japan uses magnetism to move just above the ground.

Study and design

What is the difference between science and technology? Science means studying what goes on around us to see how it works. Technology is more practical. It means designing something to do a job. Wheels, washing machines, trains, toilets and tin openers – all these exist because someone needed a better way of doing something.

Early trains had steam engines, powered by burning coal.

Wheels through history

The wheel is a great example of technology. Simple carts with wheels were first invented about 5,200 years ago. Since then, people have come up with lots more ways to use wheels. We still have simple carts – but also cars, trains, skateboards, bikes and roller coasters. We also use wheels as cogs and parts inside other machines.

A skateboard uses old technology in a new way.

This illustration of an ancient Egyptian wall painting shows a wheeled chariot.

This robot, Kismet, can interact with people.

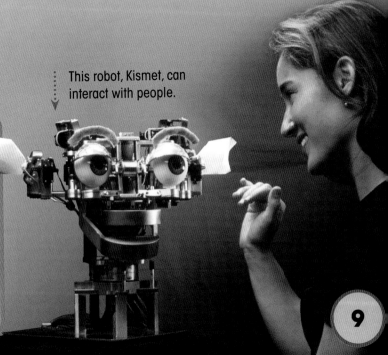

Technology with brains

We can now build smart computers and robots. Some robots can see, hear, talk and even think. One day, they could become cleverer than us.

9

Technological Inventions

This timeline shows the most important inventions in the history of technology. Follow the arrows.

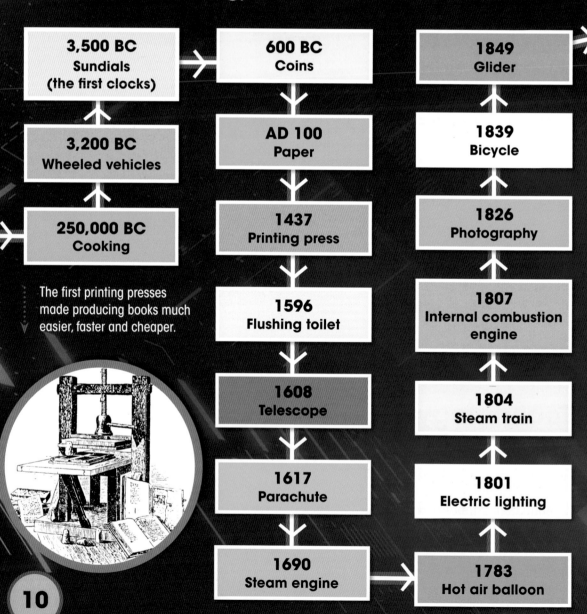

3,500 BC
Sundials
(the first clocks)

3,200 BC
Wheeled vehicles

250,000 BC
Cooking

The first printing presses made producing books much easier, faster and cheaper.

600 BC
Coins

AD 100
Paper

1437
Printing press

1596
Flushing toilet

1608
Telescope

1617
Parachute

1690
Steam engine

1849
Glider

1839
Bicycle

1826
Photography

1807
Internal combustion engine

1804
Steam train

1801
Electric lighting

1783
Hot air balloon

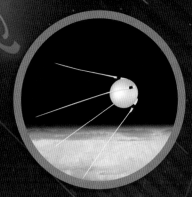

Sputnik 1, the first spacecraft, was launched in 1957.

Humans first flew in this hot air balloon in 1783, made by the Montgolfier brothers.

1854 Light bulb

1876 Telephone

1886 Dishwasher

1895 Radio

1901 Vacuum cleaner

1903 Powered aircraft

1907 Bakelite (the first plastic)

1913 Zip

1964 Computer mouse

1958 Skateboard

1957 Spaceflight

1949 Barcode

1945 Microwave oven

1944 Electronic computer

1930 Jet engine

1924 Television

1965 Touchscreen

1969 Internet

1990 World Wide Web

2015 Nanomachines

Touchscreen technology is common in today's computers and telephones.

11

Living Things

All over the world, there are billions of living things. Besides humans, there are many other animals and plants, ranging from earwigs to whales, from tiny mosses to towering trees. There are fungi such as mushrooms and tiny living things we cannot even see, such as bacteria.

African elephants are the largest animals living on land. One male African elephant can weigh as much as 90 human adults.

Large parts of our planet are covered in trees, grass, mosses and other plants.

Some creatures, like this amoeba, are too small to be seen without a microscope.

Living things can grow in all sorts of places, such as this moss growing on stone.

How Life Began

Today, there are millions of species (types) of living things on Earth. But once, there were none. How did life start? This is a big puzzle for scientists.

Life from water?

Living things need water. Some scientists think life started in a mixture of chemicals and water. Their name for it is "primordial soup". The chemicals joined to make new chemicals – the chemicals of life. They formed cells, the building blocks from which living things are gradually made. Small, simple living things appeared first.

Some scientists think that life began at the bottom of the ocean.

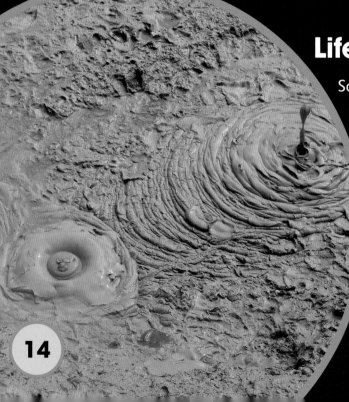

Life from mud?

Some scientists think life could have started in thick mud or clay, not in a watery "soup". They have found traces of early life-forms deep under the ground. Life could have started when chemicals in mud reacted with each other.

In some places, mud pools are heated by underground volcanic rocks. They contain lots of chemicals. Life may have started somewhere like this.

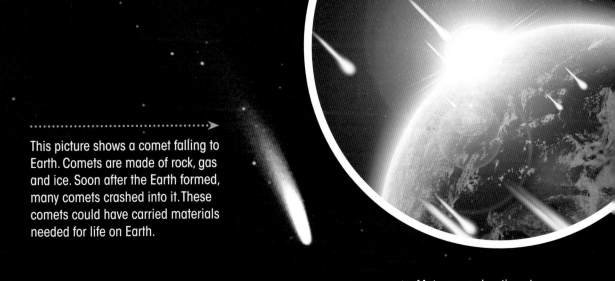

This picture shows a comet falling to Earth. Comets are made of rock, gas and ice. Soon after the Earth formed, many comets crashed into it. These comets could have carried materials needed for life on Earth.

Life from outer space?

Another idea is that life did not start on Earth. Instead, it was carried here from outer space. Comets or asteroids containing living things could have crashed into the Earth. The living things found food, water and sunlight. Slowly, life spread all over the planet. But this theory does not explain how, or where in space, life began.

Meteors or shooting stars are small pieces from comets that hit the Earth's atmosphere. They usually burn up in the atmosphere,

These stony lumps, called stromatolites, are billions of years old. They were made by simple bacteria which built up into layers. They were among the Earth's earliest life forms. The stromatolites in this picture are in Western Australia.

What are Plants?

Plants are an important type of life. They take the Sun's energy and make it into food. Without plants, most other types of life could not exist. There would be no humans, as there would be no food for us.

Green life

Plants are green because their cells contain a green chemical called chlorophyll. It allows plants to soak up the Sun's light energy. In the plant's leaves, light combines with water from the ground and carbon dioxide from the air. This process is called photosynthesis. It makes glucose, a type of sugar, as food. The plant uses glucose to build new leaves, flowers and fruits.

A leaf takes in energy from sunlight, carbon dioxide from the air and water through its stem to make food. It uses the food to build new plant parts and releases oxygen and water as waste.

How photosynthesis works

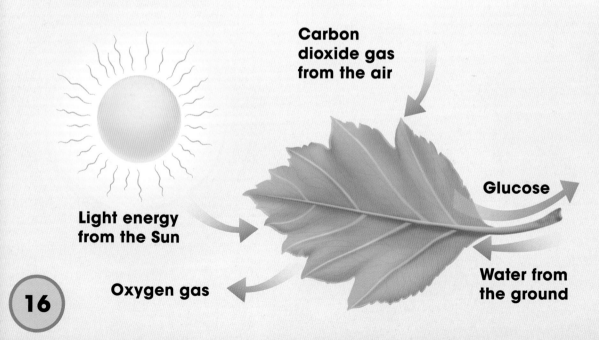

Carbon dioxide gas from the air

Glucose

Light energy from the Sun

Oxygen gas

Water from the ground

Green Earth

There are so many plants on Earth that they make large parts of our planet look green from space.

When cows eat grass, they use its energy to build their own bodies and to create milk.

Standing still

Plants cannot move from place to place. They are held in the soil by their roots, which reach for and soak up water to help the plant grow. Plants need to spread their seeds far and wide to make new plants. Some plant seeds have fluffy hairs or wings that help them float through the air.

Leaves

Stem

Roots hold a plant in one place. They also find water for the plant. Water from the soil moves into the root and then up the stem to the leaves.

Roots

Food for all

As plants grow and grow, they make lots of food. Grass, leaves, twigs, bark, fruits, seeds, nuts and flowers all become food for plant-eating animals. Then, the plant-eaters become food for meat-eating animals. In this way, plants provide food for us all.

17

What are Animals?

Animals range from tiny fleas and flies to mighty elephants and enormous whales. There are water animals, underground animals, flying animals and animals such as mice that share our homes with us. Humans are a type of animal, too.

Different cells

Like plants, animals' bodies are made up of cells. Plant cells have stiff cell walls that help plants to stand upright. Animal cells are soft. This is why many animals have bones to hold their bodies up.

Mosquitoes are flies that sometimes feed on human blood.

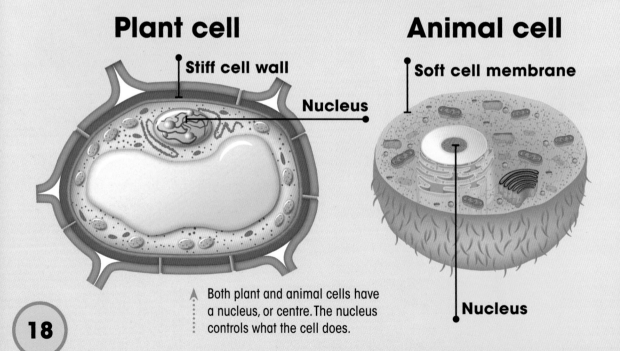

Plant cell

Stiff cell wall

Nucleus

Animal cell

Soft cell membrane

Nucleus

Both plant and animal cells have a nucleus, or centre. The nucleus controls what the cell does.

Eating

While plants soak up sunlight to live, animals have to eat. To get the energy and chemicals they need, they eat other living things. Carnivores are animals that eat other animals. Herbivores eat plants. Omnivores eat both animals and plants. Unlike plants, most animals can move around. They need to do this so that they can find food.

Rabbits (top) are herbivores and tigers (left) are carnivores. Bears (below) are omnivores – they eat many foods, including meat, fish, berries and honey.

More types of life

There are other types of living things besides plants and animals. Some people think mushrooms are plants, but they belong to another group, fungi. Fungi are not green and do not need sunlight. There are also billions of living cells called bacteria. They are too small to see without a microscope and have only one cell each.

19

Living Together

Animals, plants and other living things all depend on each other. Some are eaten by others, some need others for their food. Some types of living things help each other, while others fight each other for food, water or living space.

Places to live

Different plants and animals often share the same place to live and depend on each other to survive. Such a place is known as an ecosystem. For example, a pond is an ecosystem. It has water weeds, water insects, frogs, fish and bacteria in the water, and maybe a heron that hunts there. There are also different types of surroundings in which living things are found. They are called habitats or biomes. They include jungles, deserts, seas and the icy Arctic and Antarctic.

Frogs eat smaller animals, such as insects and snails. In turn, frogs are eaten by large fish and by birds such as herons.

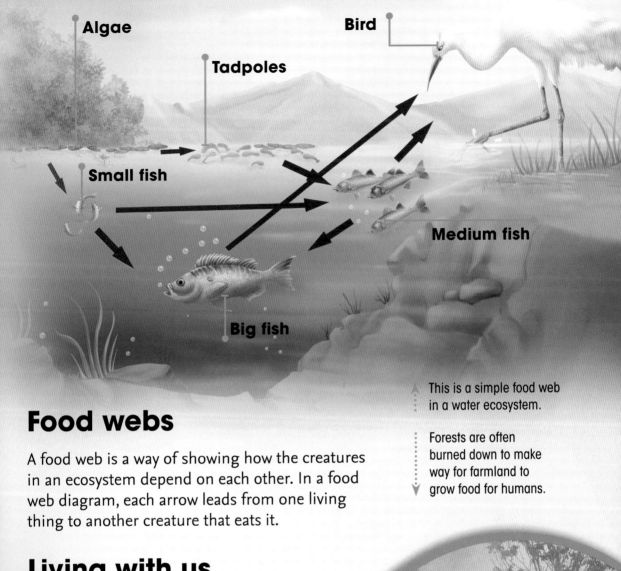

Algae

Tadpoles

Bird

Small fish

Medium fish

Big fish

This is a simple food web in a water ecosystem.

Forests are often burned down to make way for farmland to grow food for humans.

Food webs

A food web is a way of showing how the creatures in an ecosystem depend on each other. In a food web diagram, each arrow leads from one living thing to another creature that eats it.

Living with us

Humans have made a big impact on the Earth and its living things. Hunting and fishing have completely destroyed some species of living things. We have replaced some natural habitats, such as forests, with cities and farms, driving wild living things away. Pollution can also damage natural habitats and ecosystems. We can try to change this by keeping some areas wild and protecting the creatures that live there.

The Earth

We live on an amazing planet. Unlike the other planets we know of, the Earth has mainly mild temperatures. This means that most of its water is liquid, most of the time. This makes the Earth a great place for living things to survive.

The Earth itself is mostly made of rock. It has many types of rocks and minerals that are useful to us. We dig them up and use them to make all sorts of things – from houses and roads to jewellery, tools, cars and computers.

When a volcano erupts, melted rock, or lava, bursts out from inside the Earth.

The Earth's rocks form mountains and valleys.

Some minerals, such as coloured diamonds, are very rare and valuable.

Wind and water can wear away rock, creating amazing patterns.

23

How the Earth Formed

The Earth is one of eight planets that orbit, or circle, the Sun. The Sun is just one of billions of stars in our galaxy, the Milky Way. The Milky Way is one of billions of galaxies in the universe. Compared to the whole universe, our Earth is very tiny indeed.

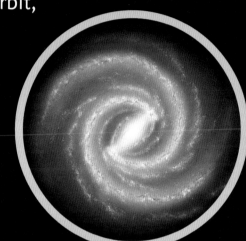

Where the Earth came from

Our Sun and the planets around it are called the solar system. The solar system formed about 4.5 billion years ago, from a spinning cloud of gas. Gases collected in the middle and formed the Sun. Around the Sun, dust and rock clumped together into balls – the planets.

▲ Our galaxy, the Milky Way, looks like swirling milk from a distance.

Sun

Mercury

Venus

Earth

Mars

Jupiter

Saturn

Uranus

Neptune

An illustration of the solar system showing the planets circling the Sun.

Inside the Earth

Lower mantle

Crust

Scientists think the Earth has a solid metal core, with molten (hot liquid) metal around it. Surrounding the core are the lower mantle and upper mantle, made of partly melted rock. Around the outside of the Earth is a crust of solid rock. The seas and oceans lie on top of the crust.

This diagram shows the layers that make up the Earth.

Molten metal

Solid metal core

Upper mantle

Stuck to the ground

We do not fall off the Earth because a force called gravity pulls us towards it. You can read more about gravity on pages 36 and 37.

The Earth's Moon

The Moon orbits, or circles, around the Earth. Experts think the Moon formed soon after the Earth did. Another planet crashed into the Earth, knocking part of it off. The broken bits clumped together into a ball (the Moon). Other planets have moons, too. Jupiter has more than 60 moons.

The Moon reflects the Sun's light. It does not have any light of its own. When only part of the Moon is in sunlight, we only see that part.

The Earth's Crust

The Earth's crust is made up of lots of different types of rock. Compared to the size of the Earth itself, the crust is not very thick. It varies from 6 kilometres (about 4 miles) to around 30 kilometres (about 19 miles) deep. It floats on top of the molten rock underneath.

Plates of rock

The Earth's crust is made up of giant sections of rock, called plates. They slowly move around and push against each other. In some places, one plate slides underneath another. In other places, new rock comes out from inside the Earth, pushing the plates apart. As the plates move, so do the continents, which are large sections of land separated by the ocean. Because of this, the shape of the Earth's land is always changing, although very slowly.

This picture shows the plates separated from each other, so you can see them clearly.

Quaking plates

As the plates push and rub against each other, they sometimes get stuck for a while. Then they suddenly slip and shake. This is what causes an earthquake.

Making mountains

When two plates push together, they sometimes make the Earth's crust crumple. The crust folds and piles up, forming lines, or ranges, of mountains. The Himalayas, the world's biggest mountain range, formed this way.

Lava comes out of an opening, called a vent, in the middle of a volcano.

Vent

When the volcano erupts, lava, rock and ash burst out.

Making volcanoes

Volcanoes form another way. Molten rock from inside the Earth breaks through a weak spot in the Earth's crust. It becomes hot, runny lava, bursting out of the Earth in a volcanic eruption. Each time this happens, lava comes out, cools, and hardens into solid rock. It piles up to form a volcano.

Lava

Strong eruptions can create smaller vents around the edge of the volcano.

Many eruptions build the volcano up into a mighty mountain.

Small vents

The Earth's Resources

The Earth's crust is not just a handy surface to live on. It is full of useful materials that we can extract, or take out, and make things with. We get fuel and energy from the Earth, too. These useful things are called resources.

Rocks and minerals

Minerals are pure substances such as diamond, silicon and salt, and metals such as gold. Rocks are mixtures of different types of minerals. Rocks and minerals have thousands of uses. We use stone for walls, pavements, roof tiles and even sculptures. We make precious stones and metals into jewellery and coins. Other metals make cars, trains and planes, pans, forks, knives, needles and millions of other everyday items.

At these salt pans in Peru in South America, salty water is left to evaporate in the sun. The water escapes into the air, leaving the salt to be collected.

A jet airplane needs lots of kerosene, a fuel made from oil from the Earth.

We mine coal from under the ground.

Energy

We need energy (see page 34) to run our vehicles, heat our homes and power electrical gadgets. A lot of energy comes from burning fossil fuels such as coal and oil. Fossil fuels are found under the ground. They are made from ancient plants and animals that got squashed down underground millions of years ago.

Living resources

Living things give us useful materials, too. For example, we use wood from trees to make houses, furniture and paper.

This house is being built of wood, which is strong and easy to use.

29

Atmosphere and Weather

The Earth is travelling through space all the time, but we cannot feel any movement. This is because the Earth is surrounded by a layer of gases, called the atmosphere. The Sun heats the Earth, and makes the air and water in the atmosphere move around. This causes weather.

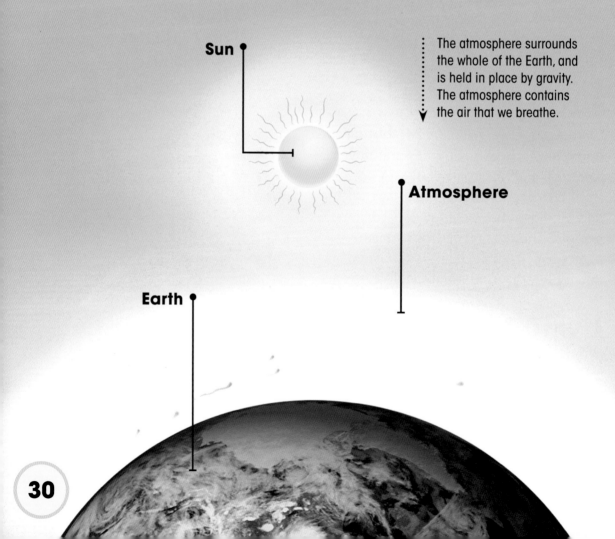

Sun

The atmosphere surrounds the whole of the Earth, and is held in place by gravity. The atmosphere contains the air that we breathe.

Atmosphere

Earth

Sun and wind

Sunshine warms the air. When air is heated up, it expands. This makes it lighter than cold air. Because of the clouds and seasons, the Sun heats some places more than others. Warmer air rises upwards, while cooler air rushes along the ground to take its place. We feel these movements of the air as wind.

Weather events, such as floods (top) and tornadoes (below), can cause a lot of damage and injury.

Water in the air

When the Sun heats the water in seas or rivers, the water evaporates. This means some of it becomes a gas and escapes into the air. It rises high into the sky. Then, as it cools down, it forms water droplets, or rain.

Climate change

Climate means the typical pattern of weather. Over many years, the Earth's climate naturally warms up and cools down. But recently, the Earth has started to warm up faster. Scientists think this is because of pollution in the air, mainly from burning fossil fuels. It is acting like a blanket, and making the Earth hotter.

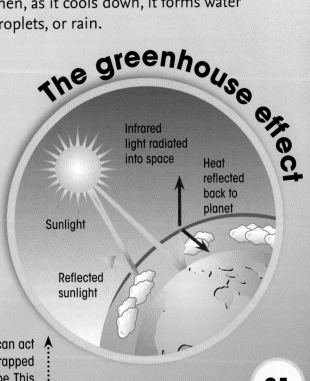

The greenhouse effect

Infrared light radiated into space

Heat reflected back to planet

Sunlight

Reflected sunlight

Pollution in the Earth's atmosphere can act like a greenhouse. Heat from the Sun is trapped close to the Earth and cannot escape. This means that the Earth gets warmer and warmer.

How Things Work

Understanding how things work is a vital part of science. It includes how things move and change shape, how light and sound travel and what happens when objects crash together. Understanding these things lets us design better machines and tools, too.

The force of gravity pulls the bike downhill. The rider can add more force by pressing down on the pedals and go even faster.

Light bulbs turn electrical energy into light energy.

Energy is also found in food. Your body turns it into other forms of energy, such as movement, heat and sound.

Solar panels collect energy from sunlight and turn it into electricity.

Energy

Energy makes everything happen. It makes machines work. It makes your body move around. It makes the Sun shine and it allows a trumpet to make a sound.

Forms of energy

Energy comes in several different forms. These include heat, light, sound and electricity. Movement is also a form of energy, known as kinetic energy. Chemical energy means the energy in substances, such as food.

Can you spot some of the forms of energy in this picture of a concert? These forms include light, heat, sound and kinetic energy.

Some foods contain more energy per mouthful than others. Do you know which of these contains the most energy? It's the chocolate.

Energy in food

Calories in food are a measure of chemical energy. If an oat bar has 100 calories, that means it will give your body 100 calories of energy – enough to run about 2 kilometres (1 mile).

Changing energy

Energy can change from one form into another. The energy stored in an object, such as a ball in your hand, is potential energy. When you throw the ball, this potential energy turns into kinetic energy, or movement energy. When you hit a drum, you turn kinetic energy into sound energy. When you switch on a light, you turn electricity into light energy.

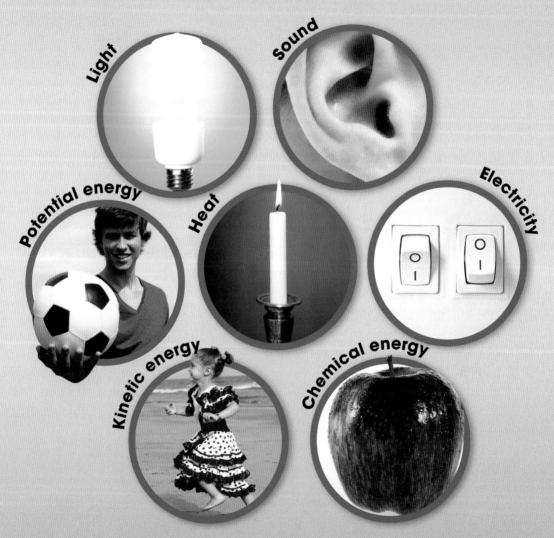

Light

Sound

Electricity

Potential energy

Heat

Kinetic energy

Chemical energy

These pictures show some of the main forms of energy.

Everlasting energy

Energy cannot be created or destroyed. The amount of energy in the universe remains the same. It just keeps changing from one form to another.

35

Forces

Forces are pushes and pulls that act on objects. Forces can make things move, stop moving, change direction or change shape.

Forces everywhere

Whenever anything moves or stops, it is because of a force. You use forces to carry a bag, catch a ball or stretch an elastic band. A crane uses force to lift heavy bricks. Objects can be moved by the force of the wind, or the pulling force of gravity.

The force of gravity pulls you down when you sit on a swing. But the swing has a force, too – it pushes upward, stopping you from hitting the ground.

You have gravity

All objects have their own gravity – even you. But it is so weak that you do not notice it. Only really huge objects, like planets, have strong gravity.

Friction

Friction is a force that slows things down or stops them from moving. It happens when two surfaces grip or slide against each other. Friction can be useful. The rubber soles on your shoes help you grip on snow and ice. Friction can also make heat. If you have cold hands, what happens when you rub them together?

Friction between rubbery trainer soles and a metal slide means you can walk up the slide.

Gravity

Gravity is an invisible force that makes objects pull towards each other. Because the Earth is very big, its gravity is very strong. It pulls objects and people towards it.

You have to take care in high places so that you do not fall. "Falling" means being pulled by the Earth's gravitational force. If there was no gravity, you would float about in the air.

Push factor

The pushing force of someone's hand makes this toy truck move.

The pushing force of the wall stops the truck.

Electricity

We use electricity to power all kinds of things, from phones, factories and washing machines to cars and computers.

What is electricity?

Electricity happens when tiny particles called electrons flow through a substance. Only some substances can conduct, or carry, electricity. Metal conducts electricity very well. Plastic and rubber do not. This is why electrical wires are made of metal – usually copper.

Collecting sunlight using solar panels is one of the cleanest ways to get electricity. When the Sun shines on the panels, it makes an electric current flow. This process does not harm the environment.

Where does electricity come from?

A machine called a generator can change a spinning movement (kinetic energy) into a flow of electricity in a wire. So we can get electricity from a spinning wind turbine or waterwheel. Another way is to burn fuel, and use it to boil water and make steam. The steam pushes wheel-shaped turbines around, and a generator changes this movement into electricity.

Lightning is a type of natural electricity.

How does it work?

Lots of gadgets and machines use electricity. When electricity flows through a narrow wire, it makes the wire heat up and glow. This is used in old-fashioned light bulbs, electric heaters, kettles, cookers and toasters. Other machines, such as an electric fan, have a motor in them. A motor is the opposite of a generator. It changes a flow of electricity into a spinning movement.

Inside an electric toaster

Heating element

Make it safe

Our bodies can conduct electricity, and it can be very dangerous. Electrical wires are covered in plastic to stop the electricity flowing into us when we touch them.

At power stations, burning fuel boils water to make steam, which pushes turbines around. The spinning movement is turned into electricity. Cooling towers (below) send waste heat back into the air as steam.

Heat

Heat is a form of energy that flows from a warm object to a cooler one. It is also called thermal energy. The hotter something is, the more energy it has.

Moving around

Heat comes from movement. Everything is made of tiny atoms and molecules (see pages 50–55). They jiggle around all the time. When an object feels warm or hot, the molecules are moving more. When an object cools down, its molecules move less. Heat energy spreads out from warmer things to colder things. The moving molecules in the warm object push against the molecules around them, making them warmer.

The thermal picture on the right shows the heat in this building. The red colour shows the hottest spots and the blue areas are the coldest.

28-01-2011   15:47

-3 -2 -1 0 1 2 3 4 5 6 7 °C

Temperature

Temperature is a measurement of how hot something is. A glass thermometer contains a coloured liquid. As the liquid warms up, it takes up more space. This makes it rise up the tube and show a higher temperature.

········· ➤
This thermometer is showing a temperature of 32°Celsius.

Growing and shrinking

When molecules move more, they push against each other more, and spread out. They take up more space. This means that when objects and substances warm up, they usually expand. When they cool down, they shrink.

Try it out

Try this test with a blown-up balloon. First put it in the fridge for ten minutes, then measure around the widest part using a tape measure. Then put it in a warm place, like a sunny windowsill, for ten minutes. Does it change size?

⋮
↓
Measure the balloon like this.

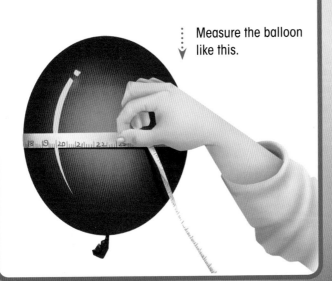

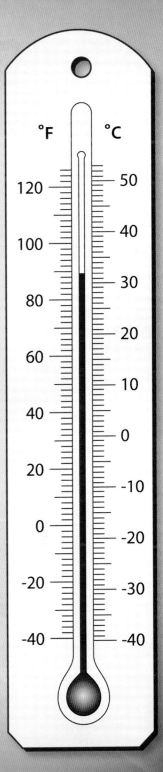

Sound

Sound is a huge part of most people's lives. Without it we could not hear each other talk, or listen to music on the radio. Sound is a form of energy.

How sound works

Sounds are made by objects shaking back and forth, or vibrating. This picture shows what happens when a guitar makes a sound.

When you pluck a guitar string, it vibrates back and forth very fast.

The string passes these vibrations into the air around it.

The vibrations travel through the air as sound waves.

Ears detect sound waves and hear the sound.

Decibels

The more energy a sound contains, the louder it is. Very loud sounds can damage our ears. The volume, or loudness, of sound is measured in decibels (dB). Quiet whispering is about 25 decibels. A loud pop concert is about 120 decibels.

People who work with loud machines wear ear defenders to protect their ears.

What stops sound?

Sound waves can spread through water, walls and other substances, as well as air. But they cannot spread through a vacuum. A vacuum is a completely empty space. There are no molecules in it, so the sound waves cannot be passed on because they have nothing to vibrate through.

In this experiment, a ringing alarm clock is put in a glass jar. The air is pumped out of the jar. This makes a vacuum inside. The bell goes quiet. You can still see it ringing, but not hear it.

Light

Light is a form of energy that we can see. Light waves spread out from a glowing object, such as the Sun or a light bulb. We see all the things around us because our eyes sense the light waves bouncing off them.

Straight lines

Light waves travel in straight lines. That is why objects cast shadows. Light cannot bend around the object, so there is a dark area where the light cannot reach.

We can only see things if they glow with light, or if light bounces off them. That is why we cannot see in total darkness.

Shadow where there is no light

Light travels in straight lines

Hand blocks the light

Light source

Refraction

Light can change direction when it bounces, or reflects, off a surface. It also changes direction when it passes from one substance, such as air, into another, such as water. This is called refraction.

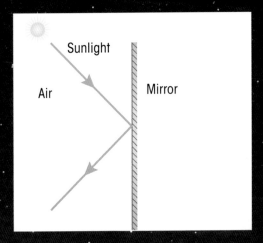

Light changes direction as it reflects off a mirror.

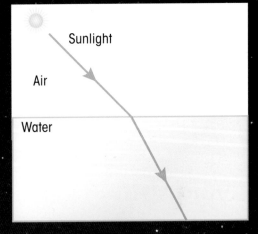

Light bends as it passes from air into water.

Super speed

Light moves very fast. It zooms through the air at just over one billion (1,000,000,000) kilometres per hour (about 621,400,000 miles per hour). That's so fast, it could zoom from Europe to America in less than one tenth of a second. Light from the Sun takes eight minutes to reach the Earth. Unlike sound, light can travel through empty space, too.

We can see the light from stars that are far away in space. Their light can take millions of years to reach us.

Electromagnetism

Electromagnetic energy is a form of energy that travels in waves. The energy waves wobble to and fro as they pass through the air, just as waves in water make it wobble up and down. Light is a type of electromagnetic energy. So are radio waves, microwaves in a microwave oven and infrared light that your remote control uses to send signals to your TV.

Wavelength

Wavelength means the length from one wave to the next. Electromagnetic waves come in different lengths. Some are so short, their wavelength is smaller than one atom (see pages 50–51). Some are more than 1 kilometre (0.6 mile) long. Light waves are medium-length electromagnetic waves. They are the only ones we can see. Gamma rays have the shortest wavelength. They are produced during nuclear explosions and can harm us.

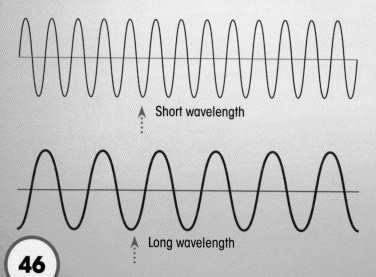

We can see different colours of light. Each colour is a slightly different wavelength. Red is the longest, and violet is the shortest. When we see white light, we are seeing all the light wavelengths mixed together.

⋏ Short wavelength

⋏ Long wavelength

You can imagine electromagnetic waves like waves in water.

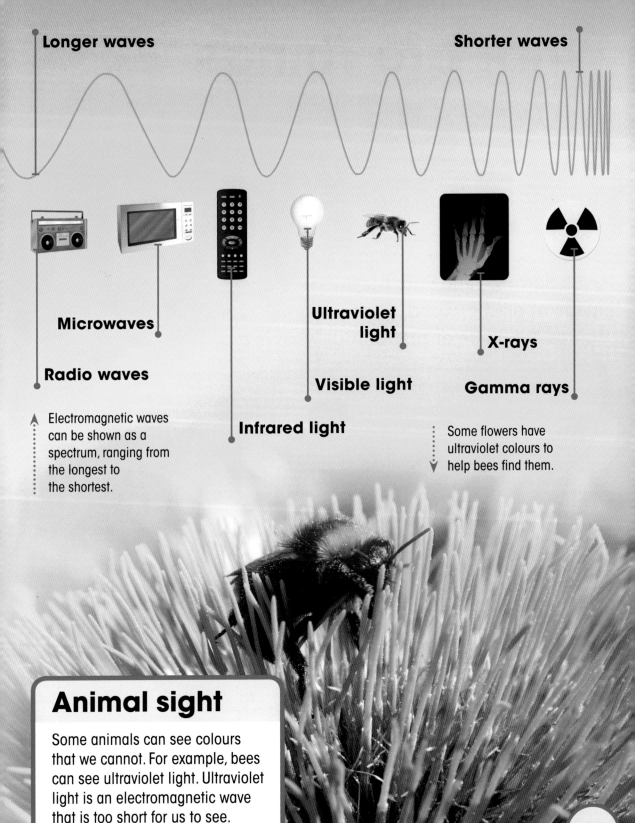

Longer waves

Shorter waves

Microwaves

Radio waves

Electromagnetic waves can be shown as a spectrum, ranging from the longest to the shortest.

Infrared light

Ultraviolet light

Visible light

X-rays

Gamma rays

Some flowers have ultraviolet colours to help bees find them.

Animal sight

Some animals can see colours that we cannot. For example, bees can see ultraviolet light. Ultraviolet light is an electromagnetic wave that is too short for us to see.

What are Things Made of?

Scientists have a name for what things are made of. They call it "matter." Everything around you is made of matter. This book is made of matter and so are your clothes – and you. Maybe you can see things made of plastic, wood, glass or concrete. All of these things are made of matter. But what is matter?

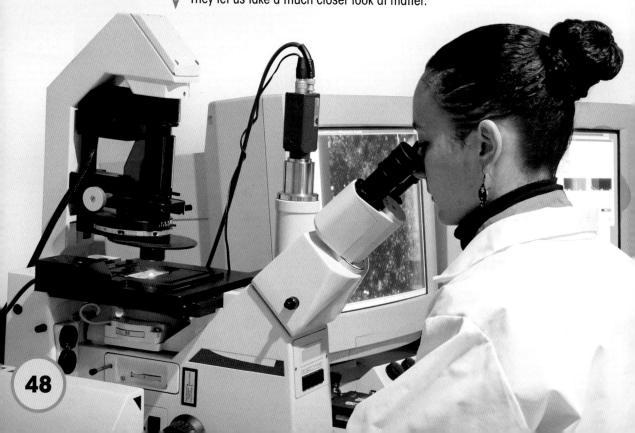

Microscopes are instruments that make tiny, invisible things look large enough to see. They let us take a much closer look at matter.

Matter can change shape – water is liquid matter.

Water that is frozen into ice is solid matter.

You can't always see matter. The water vapour, or gas, coming from this boiling pan is made of matter. It is not always easy to see.

Atoms and Molecules

All matter, or stuff, is made of tiny parts called atoms. Everything is made of atoms – mountains, water, food, computers, buildings, planets and stars. Even your body is made of atoms.

What is an atom like?

An atom is a very small piece of matter. It is a bit like a tiny ball. There are about 100 different types of atom. The different types of atom are all different sizes. They are all still tiny though – too small to see without a microscope. Each type of atom makes one type of matter, called an element.

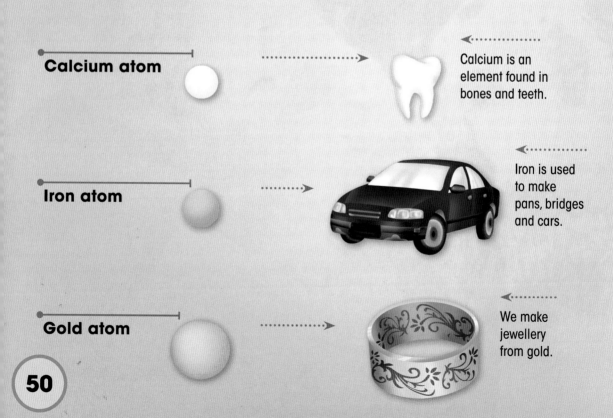

Calcium atom

Calcium is an element found in bones and teeth.

Iron atom

Iron is used to make pans, bridges and cars.

Gold atom

We make jewellery from gold.

Teeny tiny atoms

Atoms are really, really small. A piece of paper, or a page in a book, can be one million atoms thick. If you cup your hands together with some air inside, you'll be holding more than 1,000,000,000,000,000 atoms – a thousand million million.

............➤

We can see real atoms using a strong microscope. These are gold and carbon atoms.

Carbon atoms

Gold atoms

Carbon dioxide gas makes bubbles in a fizzy drink.

Molecules

Atoms often join together to make bigger parts, called molecules. Some molecules are made up of just one type of atom. Others are made up of different types of atoms joined together.

If you could look very closely at your body, you would see that it is made of many types of atoms and molecules.

Two oxygen atoms

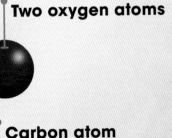

............➤

Two oxygen atoms make up an oxygen molecule. We breathe oxygen molecules from the air.

Carbon atom

............➤

A carbon dioxide molecule has two oxygen atoms and one carbon atom.

Molecules can contain one type of atom, or two or more types.

51

Solids, Liquids and Gases

Matter can exist in three main states: solid, liquid and gas. In each state, the molecules behave differently. Most substances can exist in all three states. They change from one state to another depending on how hot they are.

Solids

In a solid, the molecules are fixed together firmly. They jiggle back and forth, but they do not move far away from each other. When a solid is heated up enough, it melts and changes into a liquid.

Liquids

In a liquid, the molecules are not so tightly packed together. They can move around more, and swap places. This means that a liquid can be poured into a container, or it can separate into droplets. When a liquid is heated up enough, it turns into a gas.

When you boil water, it starts to change from a liquid into a gas called water vapour.

Gases

In a gas, the molecules are separate from each other. They zoom around at high speeds. A gas spreads out to fill the area it is in. Gases have no shape and are often invisible.

 Ice is water in its solid state.

 Molecules are fixed together in a set pattern.

 Water is often found as a liquid.

 Molecules flow around loosely.

 When water boils, it becomes a gas called water vapour.

 Molecules zoom around separately.

Human body temperature is about 37°Celsius. When you put chocolate into your mouth, it starts to melt.

If you leave solid ice cubes at room temperature, they will slowly melt and become liquid water.

Boiling and freezing

Liquid water boils into a gas at 100°Celsius, and freezes solid at 0°Celsius. So we think of these as the "boiling point" and "freezing point". Other substances change state at other temperatures. For example, chocolate is solid at room temperature (about 20°Celsius) but melts into a liquid at about 34°Celsius.

How Things Change

Substances not only change between solid, liquid and gas, but many also change into something completely different.

Chemical recipe

In a chemical reaction, two or more substances combine together and change. Their molecules (see pages 50–53) break down into atoms. The atoms form a new substance, or substances, by making new molecules. Here is one example.

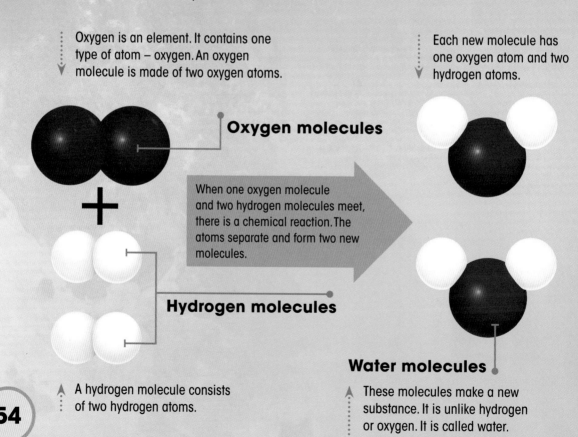

Oxygen is an element. It contains one type of atom – oxygen. An oxygen molecule is made of two oxygen atoms.

Each new molecule has one oxygen atom and two hydrogen atoms.

Oxygen molecules

When one oxygen molecule and two hydrogen molecules meet, there is a chemical reaction. The atoms separate and form two new molecules.

Hydrogen molecules

Water molecules

A hydrogen molecule consists of two hydrogen atoms.

These molecules make a new substance. It is unlike hydrogen or oxygen. It is called water.

Chemical reactions

Chemical reactions are happening around us, all the time. We use them to make things such as paints, shampoo or plastic. They happen when we cook food or burn fuel. They happen inside our bodies, too.

A scientist tries out different chemical reactions to make new chemicals to use in medicines.

See a chemical reaction

To see two chemicals reacting together, try this experiment with cooking ingredients. Make sure you do it outdoors or in a sink. Put three tablespoons of vinegar into a glass or jar. Tip in one teaspoon of bicarbonate of soda (baking soda). These chemicals react together with a lot of fizzing and foaming. One of the things they make is carbon dioxide gas. You can see it forming frothy bubbles.

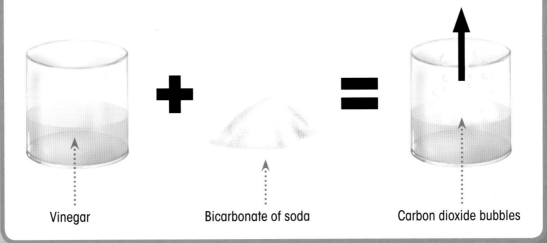

Vinegar   Bicarbonate of soda   Carbon dioxide bubbles

Technology Around Us

Humans have always invented new machines and created new ways of doing things. We have been using technology for many thousands of years. The more time passes, the more things we invent. Today, we have machines for doing all sorts of jobs, from peeling potatoes to investigating distant planets. Technology lets us chat to someone on the other side of the world, make our own movies or fly through the sky.

Communication satellites beam TV channels into our homes.

Modern technology lets all of these people chat in a meeting, even though one of them is far away in another country.

We use all sorts of gadgets and inventions at home to make household chores easier.

As technology advances, amazing new things become possible – such as using our laptop computers to do our work even if we are travelling on an airplane or in an underground train.

57

At Home

Housework used to take so long, people spent all day doing it. Or they had servants to do it for them. Technology has changed that. We have invented machines to do all sorts of housework, such as cleaning, cooking and washing clothes and dishes.

Dust buster

Instead of sweeping with a brush, a vacuum cleaner sucks up dust and dirt. It was invented around 150 years ago. Early vacuum cleaners were hand-powered, but now they are electric. A fan inside sucks the dirt up.

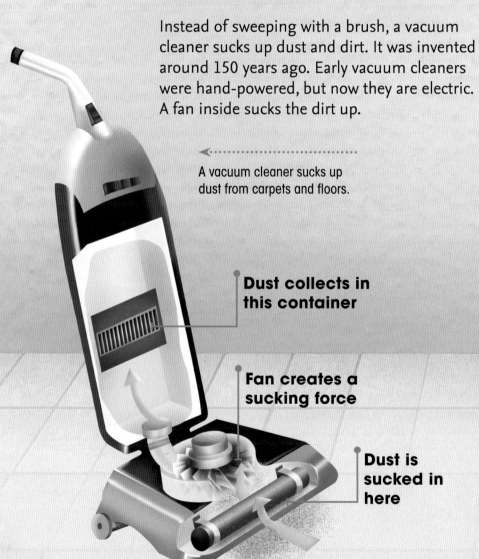

A vacuum cleaner sucks up dust from carpets and floors.

Dust collects in this container

Fan creates a sucking force

Dust is sucked in here

Machine washing

Clothes-washing machines have been around for more than 200 years. The first ones were tub-shaped, with a handle to stir the clothes. An American woman, Josephine Garis Cochran, invented the first successful dishwasher in 1886. She hated washing dishes and decided to make the job easier.

Modern dishwashers use less water and energy than dishwashing by hand.

Edison's first phonograph, or sound-recording machine.

Making music

The great inventor, Thomas Edison, invented sound recording in 1887. He found that he could use sound vibrations (see page 42) to make a needle vibrate. He made the shaking needle scratch a shaky line in a foil surface. Then he could run the needle through the groove again to make it vibrate, and play the sound back. Since then, we've invented many more ways to record sound.

Technology, like your smartphone, lets you listen to music wherever you are.

At School

Technology can be brilliant for schoolwork. Schools try to buy the best technology they can to make learning easier and better.

A world of information

The internet has probably changed learning more than any other technology. It links computers together, using phone wires, cables or wireless signals. This means you can look at information stored on other computers around the world. It is great for finding out facts, checking how to make things, looking at maps or hearing real sounds like animal calls.

Teachers no longer have to write with chalk on a blackboard. Today, most classrooms have an interactive whiteboard. A projector sends images from a computer on to a white surface. An interactive whiteboard can sense touch, so you can use your fingers on it like a pen.

Helpful technology

If you are disabled, learning at school can be extra difficult. Technology can help. For example, if you cannot see, you can use a computer to turn written text into spoken words – or into Braille writing that you can feel. If you can't hear, some schools have a system in which the teacher's voice can be sent to your hearing aid as a radio signal. People who find handwriting difficult can use a computer and keyboard instead.

It is important to have computers at school, so that everyone learns how to use them.

Check carefully

Information on the internet is not always correct. It is important to learn how to double-check facts, and find reliable websites.

You can use the internet to find lots of different types of information for a school topic.

Penguin

At Play

There is a lot of technology in the toys you have at home. Adventure playground games are full of technology, too. When you look at them, you can see the laws of science at work.

As gravity pulls on you, you zoom down a zipwire faster and faster.

Playground forces

A seesaw is a simple lever with a pivot in the middle. When you push one end down, the other end lifts up. A zipwire works using the pulling force of gravity. When you jump off the platform, the Earth's gravity pulls you downwards and along the sloping cable. A roundabout creates centrifugal force, which throws you outwards.

As a roundabout spins around, your body tries to keep going in a straight line and tends to fly off the side. You have to hold on tight to stay on.

Computer games

Computers are very important – we use them to store information, track money, design buildings and even control aircraft. But they are great to play games on, too. When you play a computer game, you press buttons on a hand-held remote to control moving pictures on a screen, using electrical signals. Some game systems even sense where you are, by shining light beams across the room. You control the game by moving your body.

Game controllers send signals to the console when you press the buttons.

Silly putty

Silly putty is a strange substance. You can bounce it, snap it and mould it into shapes. If you leave it, it melts into a puddle! Scientists invented it in the 1940s. They were trying to make a useful new type of rubber. Then they realised it would make a great toy, instead.

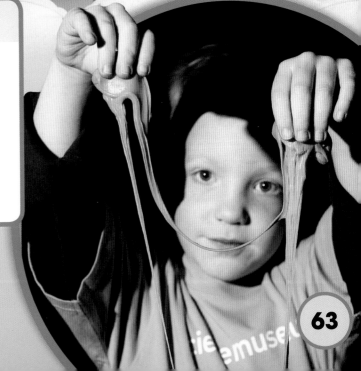

Silly putty can do many things. It can drip like a liquid and bounce like a ball.

On the Move

We are used to being able to zoom around at high speed, thanks to transport technology. Since ancient times, new inventions have made transport faster and safer.

Internal combustion engine

Cars, motorbikes, buses and lorries contain internal combustion engines. They were invented in the 19th century. By 1900, the first cars were on the road. Now, there are more than one billion. Cars make it easy to get around. Unfortunately, their engines also put pollution into the air, such as the smoke in the picture on the right. Inventors are working on new, cleaner types of cars.

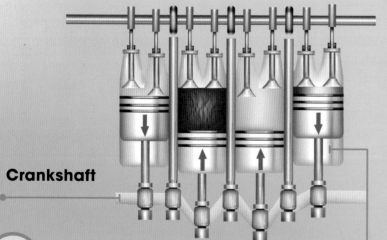

Crankshaft

Fuel chambers

Cars are powered by internal combustion engines. These engines work by burning fuel in several separate chambers. As fuel enters each chamber, it explodes, making a pushing force. The force pushes a crankshaft around, and this turns the wheels of the car.

The shape and angle of an airplane's wings allows it to fly. When air goes over a wing, the air speeds up and is pushed downwards. This creates a force that lifts the plane upwards.

Flying high

The first flying machine was the hot air balloon, in 1783. The first airplane flew in 1903. It stayed in the air for only 8 seconds, travelling about 33 metres (120 feet). Today, you can fly to the opposite side of the world in less than 20 hours.

A Segway has two wheels side by side.

Mini movers

We can save money, energy and pollution by using smaller, one-person vehicles. New mini vehicles, such as powered scooters and Segways, have an electric battery that can be recharged.

A YikeBike is a small, folding electric bike.

Air and Water

We are surrounded by air and water. We need drinking water to survive and air to breathe. We can use air and water to get the electricity we need, too.

Clean water

When you turn on the tap, fresh, clean water comes out. That only happens because of amazing technology. Water is pumped from reservoirs or rivers into treatment plants. These treatment plants filter water through layers of stones and add chemicals to kill germs. The water is carried to your house along mains pipes that run down each street under the ground.

Air conditioning

Air conditioning cools down air inside buildings and cars. This technology makes life more cool and comfortable in hot places.

At this water treatment plant, water is being cleaned in a filter tank.

Wind power

Windmills have been used since ancient times to power machines. Traditional windmills were built to grind grain into flour. Today, modern windmills, or wind turbines, generate electricity. Usually, we put lots of turbines together on a hilltop, or out at sea. This makes a "wind farm" that can provide a lot of electricity.

These wind turbines turn the movement of the wind into electrical energy.

Giant dams

Water can also turn turbines to generate electricity. The turbines capture the movement of water as it flows downhill in a river, to and fro with the tide, or up and down in waves. We get the most electricity from hydroelectric dams. The dam blocks a river, creating a lake. The water is then channelled through turbines in the dam.

The water rushing through this hydroelectric dam will be used to make turbines spin and electricity flow.

Useful Words

asteroids Lumps of rock and metal that orbit around the Sun.

atoms Tiny units from which all matter is made.

biomes Types of surroundings that living things can be found in.

Braille A writing system that allows people who cannot see to read by touching letters and numbers made of raised dots.

cells Very small units from which living things are made.

centrifugal force A force that acts outwards on a rotating body.

chemicals Substances, especially those that only contain one type of molecule.

climate change Long-term change in weather patterns.

comets Clumps of dust, ice and gas that orbit around the Sun.

conducts Carries or transmits heat or electricity.

core The central part of something, such as the Earth.

crankshaft A shaft with one or more cranks, to which the connecting rods are attached.

crust The rocky outer layer of the Earth.

electric current A flow of electricity through a substance.

electronic A word for machines that use electrical signals to work.

electrons Tiny parts of an atom.

energy The power that makes things work or happen.

evaporates To turn from a liquid into a gas.

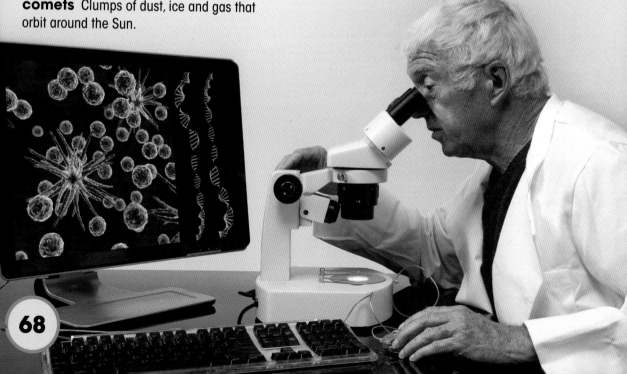

fossil fuels Fuels formed from the remains of living things.

friction A force that makes things slow down when they grip or slide against each other.

fungi A group of living things including mushrooms and moulds.

galaxy A huge cluster of billions of stars.

gas A state of matter in which molecules are spaced far apart and move very quickly.

germs Small living things, such as bacteria, that can cause diseases.

gravity A force that makes things pull towards each other.

habitats Places in which living things are found.

hydrothermal vents Cracks in the seabed that pump out hot water.

infrared light A type of light wavelength too long for humans to see.

lava Molten rock that escapes from the Earth in a volcanic eruption.

lever A bar resting on a point.

mantle A layer of partly melted rock inside the Earth.

microscope A machine that makes tiny objects appear much bigger.

microwaves A type of electromagnetic energy.

molecules Units of a substance, made up of atoms.

natural selection The way living things that are better suited to their surroundings are more likely to survive.

nucleus part of a cell that contains the matter that controls the characteristics and growth of the cell.

periodic table A chart that groups all the different elements according to their similar properties.

pollution Dirt or unhealthy substances released into our surroundings.

radio waves A type of electromagnetic wave that can be used to carry sounds.

turbine Machine that turns spinning movement into an electricity supply.

ultraviolet light A type of light with a wavelength too short for humans to see.

wavelength The length of a wave from one wave tip to the next.

Index

Published by Collins
An imprint of HarperCollins Publishers
Westerhill Road
Bishopbriggs
Glasgow G64 2QT
www.harpercollins.co.uk

First published 2011
Second edition 2013
Third edition 2016
Copyright © Q2AMedia 2011

Collins® is a registered trademark of HarperCollins Publishers Ltd

All rights reserved. No part of this publication may be reproduced, stored in a retrieval system, or transmitted, in any form or by any means, electronic, mechanical, photocopying, recording or otherwise without the prior permission in writing of the publisher and copyright owners.

The contents of this publication are believed correct at the time of printing. Nevertheless the publisher can accept no responsibility for errors or omissions, changes in the detail given or for any expense or loss thereby caused.

HarperCollins does not warrant that any website mentioned in this title will be provided uninterrupted, that any website will be error free, that defects will be corrected, or that the website or the server that makes it available are free of viruses or bugs. For full terms and conditions please refer to the site terms provided on the website.

A catalogue record for this book is available from the British Library

ISBN 978-0-00-816918-3

10 9 8 7 6 5 4 3 2 1

Printed in China by R R Donnelley APS Co Ltd.

Collins Bartholomew, the UK's leading independent geographical information supplier, can provide a digital, custom, and premium mapping service to a variety of markets.
For further information:
Tel: +44 (0)208 307 4515
e-mail: collinsbartholomew@harpercollins.co.uk
Visit our website at: www.collins.co.uk   www.collinsbartholomew.com

If you would like to comment on any aspect of this book, please contact us at the above address or online.
e-mail: collinsmaps@harpercollins.co.uk

Author: Anna Claybourne
Editor: Jean Coppendale
Project Manager: Shekhar Kapur
Art Director: Joita Das
Designers: Ankita Sharma, Deepika Verma, Jasmeen Kaur,
          Ravinder Kumar and Souvik Mukherjee
Picture Researchers: Akansha Srivastava and Saloni Vaid

For the Publisher: Elaine Higgleton and Ruth O'Donovan

Managing Editor: Alysoun Owen
Editor: Jill Laidlaw

MIX
Paper from
responsible sources
FSC™ C007454
www.fsc.org

FSC™ is a non-profit international organisation established to promote the responsible management of the world's forests. Products carrying the FSC label are independently certified to assure consumers that they come from forests that are managed to meet the social, economic and ecological needs of present and future generations, and other controlled sources.

Find out more about HarperCollins and the environment at
www.harpercollins.co.uk/green

Image credits

Cover Image: MikhailSh / Shutterstock.com

t=top, c=centre, b=bottom, tr=top right, tl=top left, tc=top centre, cr=centre right, cl=centre left, br=bottom right, bl=bottom left.

AP Photo: Franka Bruns P60; **Bigstock**: Archana Bhartia P3(tl); Philip Lange P8(t); Judy Dillon P12-13; Jim Lopes P13(t); Jonathan Nightingale P15; Ivan Kmit P17(c); Alessandro Innamorati P18(bl); Matt Cole(br); Gilles DeCruyenaere P19(t); Rykers P19(c); Kim Madrigal P20; Grondin Julien P22-23; Tomislav Zivkovic P23(c), P23(b); Andrea Danti P25(t); Michael Sheehan P29(c); Carlos Santa Maria P29(b); Julian Rovagnati P33(c); Philip Lange P33(b); Pavel Losevsky P34(b); Yanik Chauvin P35; Lars Christensen P35; Tono Balaguer P36; Saskia Massink P38(t); Ruslan Gilmanshin P39(b); Igor Shikov P47(t); Pavel Lebedinsky P47(t); Rick Lord P52; Edhar Yuualaits P57(b); Jiri Hera P59(t); Rob Marmion P61(t); Yael Weiss P61(b); Vladstock P65(t), P68-69(t); **Centers for Disease Control and Prevention**: Arthur F. DiSalvo, MD P3(cl); **Fotolia**: Railpix P8(b); Argus P15(tr); Gina Sanders P31(t); Ingo Bartussek P40; Neil Guy P47(b); KaYann P48; P49(t); Shiyana P626(t); **iStockphoto**: Nancy Nehring P13(c); Bartosz Hadyniak P28; Luminis P29(t); Vernon Wiley P37(b); John Woodcock P61(b); Gene Chutka P63(t); ScottJay P67(b); **Library of Congress**: P6; P7(t); P11(tr); **NASA**: P2-3. Reto Stockli, Nazmi El Saleous and Marit Jentoft-Nilsen, NASA GSFC P17(t); P24(t); JPL P56; **Photolibrary**: The British Library P9(t); David Nunuk/ Science Photo Library P45; **Rex Features**: Jonathan Hordle P63(b); **Science Photo Library**: Adam Jones P4(b); Sam Ogden P9(b); P10; Gustoimages P39(t); Philippe Plailly P51(t); P59(c); **Segway Inc**: P65(c); **Shutterstock**: Richard Seeley P19(b); **Thinkstock**: iStockphoto P3(cr), P3(b), P4(t), P5(cl); Comstock P5(bl); Photos. com/Getty Images P7(b); iStockphoto P9(c), P69(b); Hemera P11(tl), P11(b); Photodisc P13(b); John Foxx/ Stockbyte P14(t); iStockphoto P14(tl); Stockbyte P17(b); iStockphoto P18(t); Stockbyte P21(b); Hemera P23(t), P74; iStockphoto P24(b); Comstock P25(b); iStockphoto P31(c); Hemera P32-33, P33(t), iStockphoto P34; Comstock P34; Photos.com/Getty Images P34; Comstock P34; BananaStock P35; iStockphoto P35; Polka Dot P35; iStockphoto P35; Michael Blann/ Photodisc P35; iStockphoto P37(t); Comstock P38(b), P42, P43, Hemera P44, P56; Digital Vision P49(c); iStockphoto P49(b); Hemera P51(b); iStockphoto P53(bl); Pixland/ Jupiterimages P53(br); iStockphoto P55(t); Ryan McVay/Photodisc P57(t); Andrew Olney/Photodisc P57(c); Stockbyte P59(b); Hemera P61(b); Digital Vision P62(b); iStockphoto P64(t), P66; Digital Vision P67(t); iStockphoto P68; **YikeBike Limited**: P75(b); **Q2AMedia Art Bank**: Content, P5 (t), P6(tr), P16, P21(t), P26, P27, P30, P31(br), P37(bl), P41(bl), P43(bl), P44(b), P45(t), P46(bl), P47(t), P50, P51(bl), P53(tl), P54, P55(b), P58, P61(b), P64(b)